CONTENTS

CAN YOU TRACK DOWN BIGFOOT?

AN INTERACTIVE MONSTER HUNT

BY BRANDON TERRELL

Raintree is an imprint of Capstone Global Library Limited, a company incorporated in England and Wales having its registered office at 264 Banbury Road, Oxford, OX2 7DY – Registered company number: 6695582

www.raintree.co.uk
myorders@raintree.co.uk

Edited by Aaron Sautter
Designed by Bobbie Nuytten
Media Research by Kelly Garvin
Original illustrations © Capstone Global Library Limited 2022
Originated by Capstone Global Library Ltd
Production by Laura Manthe
Printed and bound in India

978 1 3982 3437 6

British Library Cataloguing in Publication Data
A full catalogue record for this book is available from the British Library

Acknowledgements
We would like to thank the following for permission to reproduce photographs:
Alamy: Dale O'Dell, 25, John Zada, 53; Getty Images: Bettmann, 9, 102, RichVintage, 36, Royal Geographical Society, 70; Shutterstock: Aleksey Zhuravlev, 106 (pine trees), Daniel Eskridge, 11, DCrane, 81, Dene' Miles, 12, Erik Mandre, 31, 40, Heiko Kiera, 61, Jason Eldridge, 42, JosepPerianes, 107 (mountains), mykhailo pavlenko, 50, NAM HAE WON, 96, oneinchpunch, 68, Panikhin Sergey, 92, Raggedstone, 15, RikoBest, cover, 1, sarahnev, 6, simplevect, 106-107, solarseven, cover, 1, Thierry Eidenweil, 55

ABOUT YOUR ADVENTURE

YOU are a university professor who teaches students about humans and their ancestors. In your spare time you enjoy doing research on the mysterious Bigfoot. Reports about the big ape-like beast come from around the world. You'd like nothing better than to see one in person and get proof of its existence. Will you be able to track down the legendary creature?

Chapter One sets the scene. Then you choose which path to read. Follow the directions at the bottom of the page as you read the stories. The decisions you make will change your outcome. After you finish one path, go back and read the others for new perspectives and more adventures!

Turn the page to begin your adventure.

Many researchers think that Bigfoot may be the missing link that connects modern humans to ancient apes.

SIGHTINGS!

"And that concludes today's lecture on evolution," you say, pointing to the screen behind you. On display is a photo of a human being on one side and a chimpanzee on the other.

You've just finished teaching a class about how humans and apes are related. They are both primates and have similar genes. However, they evolved differently from the same ancestor.

"What about the missing link?" one student asks curiously.

"Ah, yes," you say, rubbing your hands together. "The missing link. Are you thinking of Bigfoot?"

The student nods.

Turn the page.

"Well, unfortunately, that topic will have to wait," you say, glancing at the clock on the wall. "We've run out of time."

You're disappointed too. You know quite a bit about the search for the creature often known as the "missing link".

"Class dismissed," you say. "Have a great holiday."

It is the beginning of the spring holidays. Like your students, you look forward to some much-needed time away. You gather your own things, click off the screen and exit the now-empty classroom.

Later, at home, you think about your student's questions about Bigfoot. The study of mythical creatures – Bigfoot, the Loch Ness Monster, the Chupacabra – is called cryptozoology. You've long been interested in such things.

A poster on your wall shows a still image from the Patterson–Gimlin sighting. Two Americans, Roger Patterson and Bob Gimlin, shot the film in 1967 near Eureka, California. It's one of the clearest images ever taken of a possible Bigfoot. Patterson and Gimlin claimed to have filmed the creature lumbering into the woods.

Turn the page.

The creature in the Patterson–Gimlin film is thought to be about 2.3 metres (7.5 feet) tall.

The Patterson–Gimlin film is the main reason you joined Bigfoot Field Search & Discovery, or BFSD for short. It's a nationwide group of people trying to track down the elusive cryptid.

The BFSD website is dedicated to information and sightings of Bigfoot, and you want to have a look at it. You take a seat and open your laptop.

"Photographer spies Sasquatch on foggy nature walk in Washington State" reads the first post. The Pacific Northwest is a hotspot for Bigfoot sightings, the most in the United States.

The second post reports a sighting of a creature similar to Bigfoot in the Everglades of Florida. Known as the Skunk Ape, it has a powerful and nasty odour.

Finally, a third post says a group of hikers saw a huge furry creature in the Himalayan Mountains. They think it could be a Yeti!

Tales from Nepal and Tibet describe a huge hairy beast called a Yeti that walks on two legs like a human.

Because it's the holidays, you have some time on your hands. You've never travelled anywhere to investigate Bigfoot sightings before. But you decide it's time to change that, starting now.

You glance over the three posts and choose where in the world you'd like to go.

To fly to Washington State, turn to page 13.

To fly to the Everglades of Florida, turn to page 42.

To travel to the Himalayas in Nepal, turn to page 71.

11

The majority of reported Bigfoot sightings take place in the mysterious, foggy forests of the Pacific Northwest in the United States.

CHAPTER 2

THE FOG OF WASHINGTON

"Washington, here I come," you say. Washington State has the highest number of Bigfoot sightings – more than 650 per year! It is also the BFSD home base. You've never been to the state before. Now is a good time to head there and check things out for yourself.

You use your laptop to buy a plane ticket for the following day and begin to pack.

When you arrive in Washington, it's cold and drizzly. The minute you're off the plane, you make a phone call. The woman you call is called Mae Walton, and she is the president of BFSD.

"Hello, Mae," you say.

"Welcome to Washington!" Mae replies.

Turn the page.

"Can you tell me more about the sighting?" you ask.

"Yes," she answers. "A nature photographer was up in the hills near Downey Park when he saw a large shape in the woods. He was able to snap a couple of photos."

"Have you seen the photos?"

"I haven't had a chance to see them yet," Mae admits. "And I haven't been able to talk with him on the phone either."

You step outside the airport door and see a yellow taxi waiting. You wave it over. "I'd love to talk with you more about BFSD," you say. "But I also want to meet this photographer."

"I understand completely," Mae said. "I can give you the address for BFSD if you'd like. Or if you want to meet with the photographer, I have his information too."

Shadowy figures in dark, wooded areas may often be mistaken for a Bigfoot.

The taxi pulls up next to you. You roll your luggage around to the boot. The driver, an older man with a drooping moustache and weathered skin, gets out and helps you load your bags. He slides them into the boot carefully, then asks, "Where ya headin'?"

To visit Mae, turn to page 16.
To visit the photographer, turn to page 19.

"I'd love to visit BFSD headquarters," you tell Mae.

She laughs. "You mean my cabin in the woods? That's fine." She gives you the address. "I'll meet you out there in a couple of hours," Mae says.

You ask the taxi driver to take you to your hotel. You drop off your bags in your room and freshen up. Then you call for another taxi to take you to Mae's cabin.

Before long, you're heading down a twisting, narrow gravel lane with trees on either side. Ahead is a log cabin with warm yellow light glowing from the windows.

When you knock on the door, Mae answers it. She has her long grey hair pulled back in a ponytail. She smiles. "Come on in," she says.

Mae's cabin is filled with Bigfoot materials and photos. The walls are covered with posters. Most noticeably, you see a familiar poster showing a still image. "Hey, that's from the Patterson–Gimlin film," you say, nodding at the poster. "It's the most iconic image of Bigfoot ever captured. I have the same one."

Mae agrees. "Yeah," she says. "The way the creature strides across the frame and looks back at the filmmaker is haunting."

Mae shows you around her cabin. Her desk contains numerous sketches of Bigfoot. Most are what you expect to see: a 2-metre-tall beast with red-brown fur, long arms and a broad nose. She even has a foot mould that's carved out of alder wood.

Turn the page.

"We get a lot of reported sightings. And people often bring in evidence like bits of fur or photos of large footprints. But we have to be careful of hoaxes," she says, pointing at the wooden foot mould. "This is one way people trick Bigfoot seekers. They often make fake footprints in the mud with one of these."

You and Mae continue to discuss Bigfoot hoaxes and more current sightings until it is late. You check your watch. "I should get back to my hotel," you say. "It's been a long day. But this has been very interesting. I'm glad I came."

"Me too," Mae says. "Why don't I call that photographer, Robbie Grossman? We can meet him out near Downey Creek in the morning."

"That sounds great, thanks."

You call for a taxi and head to the hotel for a good night of rest. Tomorrow, the hunt begins.

Turn to page 22.

"I think I'd like to visit the photographer," you tell Mae. She gives you his address, and you relay the information to the taxi driver.

"I'll see you tomorrow morning at Downey Creek," Mae says.

The taxi carries you across the city. When you reach your destination, you notice the house is a modest two-storey home made of white wooden boards and with a large front porch.

You knock on the porch's screen door, and see a shadow move inside. The door opens, and a tall man in his thirties stands in the doorframe. He has a goatee, and his long black hair is tucked inside a baseball cap.

"Can I help you?" he asks.

You introduce yourself and explain that you're there to talk about his Bigfoot photo.

Turn the page.

He shakes your hand and introduces himself. "Robbie Grossman. Come in."

Robbie's house is filled with beautiful photos in black frames. One shows a moose wading in the water. Another shows a fox leaping in tall grass.

"Here's the photo I took the other day." Robbie leads you to the dining room table, where he slides a large print across to you.

The photo is blurry. It's full of trees, and hard to see much of anything. It's nothing like the Patterson–Gimlin film.

"There. See that?" Robbie points to a vague brown shape in the trees. "That must be a Bigfoot."

You're not convinced.

"I know it's not a great image," Robbie says. "But before I took it, I heard this strange grunting and gurgling. Then this thing appeared. I only just got my camera ready in time."

"Would you be up for showing me where you saw it tomorrow morning?"

Robbie nods. "Yes, I'll do that."

You glance at your watch. You decide to call it a night and phone for a taxi to return to the hotel.

"Do you think it's a Bigfoot?" Robbie asks as you wait for your taxi.

You shrug. "We'll find out," you say. "But it could just be a moose or some other animal."

The following morning is crisp and cool. When you reach Downey Creek, a layer of fog lies across the forest. Tall trees surround you as you travel down the path. A high-tech digital camera is slung around your neck, and you wear a backpack with other kit in it.

Soon, a blue jeep bounces along the path towards you. Mae gets out. "Lovely morning for a Bigfoot hunt," she says with a smile.

Turn the page.

A short time later, Robbie Grossman joins you as well.

"So, do you remember where you took the photo?" Mae asks him.

He nods and gestures. "Right this way."

Robbie leads you to a clearing. He points north to a small cluster of trees. "I heard the noises here," he says. "And I took the photo just a bit further off the path."

You spend the morning quietly discussing Bigfoot with Mae and Robbie. Meanwhile, you listen for any disturbance in the trees. You search for any sign of proof in the area. You look for footprints, fallen or broken branches, bits of coarse hair and so on. But you find nothing. Eventually, Mae says she has to leave. She asks Robbie if he'd be willing to share a copy of his photo with BFSD.

"Yeah," he says. "I need to go home now too. But I'll bring over a copy of the photo later today."

"Are you okay out here by yourself?" Mae asks you.

You nod. "I'll be fine," you reply. "I'll call if I need a lift."

Mae and Robbie drive away, leaving you alone in the woods of Downey Creek.

The place where Robbie took the photo was in this clearing. It would be the best way to get a clear view of the creature. There are dense woods all around you, though. It could be the perfect place to hide and wait for Bigfoot to show up. Now that you're alone, you must decide where to set up your stakeout.

To remain in the clearing, turn to page 24.
To travel into the denser woods, turn to page 29.

Robbie said he saw the creature in the clearing. You want to get a clear picture, so you decide to remain there for the time being. The trees are thick around you. They make the woods fairly dark, even on a sunny day. Thankfully, the layer of fog soon begins to burn off.

You remain at the edge of the clearing, crouching in the weeds. You're not afraid of Bigfoot attacking you. You know the creature is normally wary. As the hours tick by, the day slowly turns to evening. You grow tired and wonder if you should have tried a different spot.

But then you spy movement from the corner of your eye.

A shadowy shape is at the far edge of the clearing. It's tall and lean, but hard to see clearly. You try to steady your breath. Your hands are shaking as well. This could be your big chance, after all!

Sometimes shadows or dark objects in the distance may look like a creature is hiding among the trees.

You raise the camera to your eye and try to focus on the creature.

Click! Ca-click!

You peek at the photos. They aren't blurry. But they're also not much better than Robbie Grossman's. The shape is hard to see clearly under the dark trees.

You want to get closer.

To get closer, turn to page 26.
To remain where you are, turn to page 27.

You creep through the undergrowth at the edge of the clearing. The shape remains on the far side. You take a step closer. Then another . . .

SNAP!

You've stepped on a dry twig! You look down at it, then back up. The creature is gone.

"Argh!" you hiss under your breath.

You study the area and find trampled shrubbery. You also see what looks like half of a large footprint. It's hard to tell, though.

That evening, you tell Mae what you saw. You think it could be a Bigfoot, but you're not sure. You spend the remainder of your holiday in Downey Creek looking for the creature. But you don't see the shape again.

THE END

To read another adventure, turn to page 11.
To learn more about Bigfoot, turn to page 103.

If it's truly a Bigfoot in the trees, getting closer could scare it away. You decide to remain where you are and hope for a better shot.

You watch as the shape lopes between the trees. But it doesn't come out into the clearing. You take a couple of photos anyway.

After a while, the creature moves closer to you. Your knees groan in protest. You've been crouching in the bushes for a long time, and it's making you sore.

Come on, you think. *Come out into the clearing.*

It's almost like the shape heard you. It steps from the bushes into the early evening glow of the clearing.

Click! Ca-Click!

You barely have time to take a few photos before it once again disappears into the shadows.

Turn the page.

"These are fantastic!"

Mae Walton nods her head excitedly. You're back at her cabin, sharing the photos you've just taken. In them, you can clearly see a large shape with long arms and a broad chest.

"I think these will rival any other Bigfoot photo," Mae continues.

"I couldn't say for sure it was Bigfoot," you admit. "But it's definitely something . . . unexplained."

You smile broadly. These images will be used by BFSD for years, and your name will be well-known by the group.

Congratulations! Your holiday was very successful!

THE END

To read another adventure, turn to page 11.
To learn more about Bigfoot, turn to page 103.

You know Robbie saw the beast in the clearing. But you feel you might have more success deeper in the woods around Downey Creek.

You stand and walk away from the clearing and into the trees. You find a small path trampled by animals and decide to follow it.

As evening approaches you take out a small meal from your backpack. You sit with your back leaning against a thick tree trunk to eat.

As you finish, deep shadows take over the woods. Soon you hear the sound of branches snapping! Something is crashing through the forest towards you – and it sounds big!

You look up and see large branches in the tree next to you. If you climb up there, you might get a better view of whatever is moving towards you.

To climb the tree, turn to page 30.
To remain on the ground, turn to page 39.

You quickly leap up and hastily climb the tree. Whatever you heard is still lumbering your way. You can hear it grunting and puffing.

You find a solid branch to hold you and lay on your stomach. If this is Bigfoot, there's no way you're going to miss a chance to take photos of it. But it may be too dark. Still, you have to try.

Soon you notice movement near by. A shape appears between two trees, and you level your camera.

Click!

Brilliant light bursts through the trees. "Oh no, the flash!" you hiss. You quickly try to turn off the flash on your camera. But you lose your grip on the branch!

You slip off the branch and fall to the ground.

"Oof!" you exhale as the wind is knocked from your lungs.

Then you feel your ankle throb in pain. You must have twisted it in the fall.

Suddenly the creature you heard appears before you. But it's not Bigfoot. It's a giant, lumbering brown bear! You clutch your ankle in one hand and your camera in the other.

The bear suddenly rushes forwards. It's heading straight towards you!

To yell at the bear and run away, turn to page 32.

To stay still, turn to page 33.

Adult brown bears can weigh more than 270 kilograms (600 pounds) and run up to 55 kilometres (35 miles) per hour.

"Aaahhh!"

You shout and wave your arms frantically as you try to scare off the bear. Then you use your camera to take photos with the bright flash. It lights up the evening shadows and the charging bear. But your actions do nothing to stop the animal.

You turn and run.

Your ankle throbs with pain, but you can still move. Unfortunately, running from a bear is a bad idea. The last thing you hear is the bear roaring before it takes you down.

When Mae finds your camera the next day, there are no photos of a Bigfoot. Just photos of a horrifying bear attack.

THE END

To read another adventure, turn to page 11.
To learn more about Bigfoot, turn to page 103.

You try to stay calm as the bear approaches. Running will only put you in greater danger. You know that the best course of action is to remain still. The bear stops, puffs and sniffs the air around it.

You have a chocolate bar in your backpack. Maybe, if you get rid of it, you can safely slip behind the trees. Slowly, you reach into your pack until you feel the chocolate bar. You slip it out of your pack and peel off the wrapper.

With a mighty heave, you throw the chocolate towards the bear. The chocolate lands in the leaves, and the bear immediately goes after it.

You take the chance to slip behind the nearest fir tree. You hope it's enough to keep you safe. You squeeze your eyes shut and wait.

After what feels like an eternity, the bear finally lumbers away.

Turn the page.

It's nearly dark, and you're ready to get back to your hotel. But then you see another shape. This one is taller, leaner and has a more humanlike shape than the bear. You check to make sure your flash is off, then take several photos.

The shadows are deep, but it's clear you've got something important.

Click! Ca-click!

The creature warbles a gurgling sound from its throat. It heard your camera, and now it's heading in your direction!

You gather your things and take off towards the main path out of the forest. When you reach a split in the path, you can't remember which direction to go in!

To go left, go to page 35.
To go right, turn to page 36.

There's no time to think! You quickly take the path on the left and try to run from the creature at your back.

It's getting darker. You're not fleeing the woods. In fact, you're stumbling deeper into the forest. You don't see the enormous fallen fir tree crossing the path until it's too late.

WHAM!

You feel a sickening crunch as your camera's lens shatters against the tree.

But there's no time to think about it. The creature has reached you. You try to block its attack, but it's too late and you know it. All you can do is hope that someone finds your camera and the evidence of Bigfoot's existence inside it.

THE END

To read another adventure, turn to page 11.
To learn more about Bigfoot, turn to page 103.

You feel that turning right is the right way to go. You guessed correctly. The small path is the same one you took earlier that day. Only now, in the dark, it's hard to see two metres ahead of you. Your ankle aches so you slow down.

It's a good thing you do. Low-hanging spruce branches nearly cover the path. You have just enough time to swat them away and safely pass.

In the dark and shadowy woods, it may be easy to mistake a standing bear for a Bigfoot.

As you stumble down the path, you keep listening for the creature behind you. The grunting and growls have grown quiet. You turn back to check if it's still following you and –

Crack!

As you turned, your camera swung out to strike a tree. It's damaged. But in the darkness, it's hard to see how badly.

You reach the clearing where your adventure began that morning. You call Mae, and she soon arrives in her blue jeep to pick you up.

"Anything to report?" she asks when you climb into the vehicle.

In the small glow of the jeep's interior lights, you check your camera. The data card seems to be damaged. None of the photos you took are able to be seen.

Turn the page.

"No!" You slam the camera down in frustration.

"What did you see?" Mae asks.

You shrug. "I'm pretty sure I saw Bigfoot," you reply.

"What a shame – no one will ever know for sure," Mae says.

She's right. You're almost certain you saw a Bigfoot. It's too bad others won't be able to see your amazing photos.

THE END

To read another adventure, turn to page 11.
To learn more about Bigfoot, turn to page 103.

I should stay on the ground and not climb the tree, you think to yourself.

You take the time to check your camera settings. You notice the flash is still on. In this darkness, a bright burst of light would frighten away whatever is coming your way. So you switch it off. Then you crouch in the shrubbery and take some photos as the shape comes into sight.

It's not Bigfoot. It's a bear. It hasn't seen you, but your heart begins to race. You hope it hasn't smelled the food you ate or the chocolate bar that's still in your pocket.

The bear snorts and puffs, and then it begins to lumber towards you!

You hold your breath and remain crouched in the tall grass and bushes.

At the last moment, the bear stops, turns and ambles off into the trees.

Turn the page.

If you see a bear in the woods, do not try to approach it. Give it as much space as possible so it doesn't feel threatened.

You breathe a sigh of relief.

Looking at the bear photos, you realize it's much too dark to continue. You call Mae and ask her to come and get you.

As you walk along the path back to the main clearing, you hear something. A warbling kind of sound. It's unlike anything you've ever heard. Could it be the sound of Bigfoot?

You quickly turn your camera setting to video to record the noise. It continues for roughly five minutes, and you capture it all.

When Mae arrives in her jeep, you play the recording for her.

"That sounds amazing!" Mae is elated.

"Do you think it's a Bigfoot?" you ask. "Because it definitely doesn't sound like any bear or other wildlife I've ever heard before."

"We'll upload it to the BFSD website and let the world hear it," Mae says, smiling. "They'll be the judge. I'd say your trip to Washington has been pretty successful."

You agree.

THE END

To read another adventure, turn to page 11.
To learn more about Bigfoot, turn to page 103.

Everglades National Park stretches across more than 6,200 square kilometres (2,400 square miles) in southern Florida, USA.

CHAPTER 3

THE SKUNK APE OF THE EVERGLADES

"Florida, here I come!" you say. You click from the BFSD website to the airline's website to book your ticket. You've never been to Florida before, and you're excited to explore the Everglades.

As you pack, you think about the cryptid creature known as the "Skunk Ape". You know a bit about it. After all, Florida has had more than 300 combined Bigfoot and Skunk Ape sightings. It's the second-highest number in the United States. The Skunk Ape is supposedly related to Bigfoot, with a similar look and size. It's believed to be two metres tall with red-brown hair and a long face, similar to a giant orangutan. Plus, it's called the Skunk Ape for good reason – it stinks!

Turn the page.

Your plane lands in Fort Myers, Florida, early in the morning. You can tell it's going to be a scorching day. You rent a car and head off into the Everglades. Occasionally, you see an alligator or two basking in the sun in a ditch by the road.

Finally, you arrive at your destination: Gator Jim's Boat Tours! It's a rickety building of faded wood. At the entrance, you're welcomed by a large statue of an alligator wearing a straw hat and a wide grin.

The building sits next to a small inlet of water. Multiple airboats wait at the docks. Several tourists are lined up to take a tour. You approach the building, where a woman sells tickets.

"Can I help you?" she asks.

"I'm looking for Jim," you say.

"That'd be me!" a lively voice says behind you.

You turn to see a man with a scruffy beard and a wide smile. You introduce yourself to Jim and explain the reason for your visit. "I'm here because of the Skunk Ape sighting."

"Oh, that ol' thing?" Jim walks off and waves for you to follow. "Lemme show you where I saw him."

He leads you to an airboat, and you climb aboard. Jim flicks some switches, and the propeller whirs to life. Soon the boat glides off into the water. Jim steers the boat into the Glades, taking turn after turn among the trees and marshland. Eventually, he slows down.

"Saw it right in there." He points to a small group of trees on what appears to be dry land.

You're ready to start your search.

To remain in the glades alone, turn to page 46.
To stay with Jim on the boat, turn to page 64.

"It looks pretty dry over there," you say. "Dry enough for me to wander around alone for a bit?"

"Sure enough," Jim says. "But beware of the wildlife. We're out past the tour boundaries. Not many boats venture out this far."

You nod. "I can manage."

You step off the boat carefully. Your boots sink just a bit into the spongy earth. As you walk out into the marsh, Jim says, "I'll be back to get ya in a few hours."

Then he's gone, and you're all alone.

You explore the area and discover a rocky outcropping to your left. To your right is the marshy field where Jim saw the Skunk Ape.

To head towards the rocky outcrop, go to page 47.
To walk into the marshy field, turn to page 49.

The rocky area isn't where Jim saw the cryptid, but it looks like the ideal place to begin your search. Plus, it'll give you a great perch for taking photos.

You slowly make your way through the marsh, thankful for the tall boots you're wearing. Each step squelches as you trudge through the marshland.

You reach the rocks and begin to climb. But something stops you.

"Wait a second," you mutter. A mud-covered area on the rocks to your left appears out of place. "What could that possibly be?" you ask yourself.

Your voice sounds loud in the relative quiet of the Glades. You walk over to examine the muddy patch of rocks.

"Well, I'll be . . ." you whisper.

Turn the page.

What appear to be large handprints cover a section of the rocks. The handprints are much larger than your own. The fingers are twice as long as a normal human's fingers.

You take multiple photos of the handprints. You also take some close-ups with your hand in the frame for size reference. Your heartbeat races. This is an amazing discovery.

Suddenly, there is movement at your feet. You jump back, startled. You've been so focused on the handprints, you've neglected the area around you.

A large, slithering python approaches. If you climb the rocks, you could ruin the handprints. But if you don't, you don't know what will happen with the snake.

To climb the rocks, turn to page 60.
To fend for yourself against the snake, turn to page 63.

The marshy field is where Jim thinks he saw the Skunk Ape, so that's where you'll begin your search. You trudge across the marshes, thankful for your thick, tall boots.

Movement catches the corner of your eye, and you turn to see several deer loping between the trees. You spy other wildlife, including a curious raccoon. But nothing that looks like a giant orangutan.

You find a dry spot in the marsh where you can rest. It's also the perfect spot to watch for anything unusual. Plus, Jim warned you to remain vigilant about dangerous wildlife.

For several hours, you stay crouched in the marsh. The sun continues to beat down on you from a cloudless sky. You wipe sweat from your forehead. Your legs feel like rubber, and you're not sure how much longer you can stay out here. Jim should be arriving in his airboat soon.

Turn the page.

Many species of wildlife make their home in the Everglades' thick trees and swampy marshes.

Crack!

A branch nearby snaps, startling you. Your eyes dart back and forth. Could it be Jim returning for you? But you don't hear the whir of the airboat propeller.

There! You see something to your left in the trees beyond the open marshland. It's a tall shape. It looks somewhat like a human.

To follow the humanlike shape, go to page 51.

To watch from a distance, turn to page 54.

You're exhausted from crouching in the sun all morning. But this is the first chance you have to get a photo of the cryptid creature. You're not passing up that chance!

You quickly stand to get your bearings. But your legs ache, and a numb feeling shoots through them as soon as you stand up. You need a minute to recover.

Luckily, the shape in the trees doesn't seem to have noticed you. You creep closer, bringing your camera to your eye to snap off a couple of shots.

You check the photos in the camera's screen. They're blurry. "Aaahh," you hiss. You need to get closer.

With stealth in mind, you continue to close in on the shape. It's still hidden among the trees.

What is it? you wonder. Could it really be a Skunk Ape?

Turn the page.

You're paying so much attention to the creature that you don't watch where you're walking. A twisted root reaches out of the ground like a claw. You don't notice and step into it. You topple forwards and fall into the mucky marsh with a loud *splurch*!

You quickly scramble to your feet. Mud coats your camera. The muck smears across the lens and the view screen.

Worse yet, when you look into the trees, you see that the mysterious shape is no longer there. Your fall into the muck scared it away.

Disappointed, you walk over to where the shape had been hiding. You just see trees, mud and –

"Wait a second!"

At your feet, there in the mud, is a huge footprint!

Researchers often make plaster moulds of what they believe are footprints left behind by Bigfoot.

You have the materials in your pack to create a plaster mould. You mix the plaster and pour it into the muddy print, making a mould.

When the mould hardens, you remove it. It's perfect!

By the time Jim returns, you have a plaster cast of the print, along with some grainy photos. You can't wait to share your find with BFSD!

THE END

To read another adventure, turn to page 11.
To learn more about Bigfoot, turn to page 103.

You've been crouching in the sun all morning. This is your first chance to get some photos of a possible cryptid. There's no way you're going to try getting closer and risk scaring it away.

You remain in the marshy grass, snapping photos from a distance. You check the view screen. The images are blurry. It's hard to tell what the shape could be.

You see a pool of water to your left. You think you might be able to get a better angle on the mysterious creature from there. So you begin to crawl in that direction.

It's slow-going, but eventually you're next to the water. You wipe your muddy hands on your trousers and make sure your camera is not covered in mud. Your leg muscles are burning from the effort of slogging through the marsh.

Thankfully, the shape is still there. You ready your camera, focus in on the shape and –

Splash!

What was that? you think.

You forget about the mysterious shape for a moment. You spin round to see that something is in the water, swimming towards you.

It's a huge alligator!

To freeze in place, turn to page 56.
To attack the gator, turn to page 58.

American alligators can grow up to 4.6 metres (15 feet) long and weigh as much as 454 kilograms (1,000 lbs).

The alligator is 6 metres away. It hasn't seen you yet.

The marsh is thick. If you tried to run, you would be slow and unsteady. The alligator would easily overtake you. Instead, you decide the best thing to do is freeze in place.

Your heart thunders in your chest, and you hold your breath. For a brief moment, you believe the alligator will swim past you.

But then it turns in your direction!

Oh no! Your voice screams in your head. *I need to get away!*

The alligator slithers through the dark water towards you.

You turn and run. The mud bogs you down. It feels like you're going in slow motion. The alligator snaps its jaws, sliding out of the water in pursuit.

You duck behind a clump of tall grass. This is it. You didn't expect your adventure to turn out this way. You close your eyes and wait for the end.

But suddenly a putrid stench fills the air, and a loud growl echoes across the marsh. There's a lot of thrashing and hissing sounds, and then . . . silence.

You peel your eyes open. The alligator has gone. You can't believe it. Although you don't have any proof, you're sure it was the Skunk Ape who saved you.

One thing is for sure. You'll be glad when Jim picks you up, because you're never coming back out to the Glades again!

THE END

To read another adventure, turn to page 11.
To learn more about Bigfoot, turn to page 103.

The alligator is 6 metres away from you, and it hasn't seen you yet. You could try to run away as fast as you can. But the marsh is thick. If you ran, you would be too slow. The Glades are home to the alligator. It would easily catch you.

However, you can't just stand here. You have to defend yourself.

You slowly crouch down and scoop up a large branch in one hand. Your heart thunders in your chest. You hold your breath as the alligator continues to swim nearer. For a brief moment, you think it will swim away.

But then it turns in your direction!

This is it! The alligator slides out of the water and heads towards you. You grip the branch with both hands like a baseball bat. You hold it over your head and swing down hard.

THWACK!

You hit the alligator square in the snout. It looks stunned, but it continues forward.

"Take this!" You swing again, hitting it even harder.

The second blow does the trick! The frustrated alligator turns and slips back into the water, swimming away.

You look down. In all the commotion, you didn't notice that your camera had fallen into the swamp. You're certain it'll be useless now.

Still, when Jim picks you up later that day, you tell him what you saw. You're convinced that you saw a Skunk Ape. And the fact that you're leaving the Glades with your life is victory enough.

THE END

To read another adventure, turn to page 11.
To learn more about Bigfoot, turn to page 103.

The snake slithers closer. You could try to attack it, but that seems dangerous. The only real answer is to climb the rocks and hope you get out of the snake's range.

You begin to slowly make your way up the rocks. As you climb, the snake creeps onto the rock you were just standing on. Beside you are the muddy handprints of the Skunk Ape. You're disappointed, but to escape the snake, you'll have to crawl over the handprints. You try to be careful, but the knees of your trousers smudge and smear the handprints.

So much for actual proof, you think. Your photos of the handprints will now be the only evidence.

Your mind shifts quickly from what is lost to what is at your back. You think of the snake wrapping round you and squeezing the life from you before swallowing you whole.

You move faster.

You stand and leap from the rock you're on to the one above you. By reaching it, you'll likely be out of the snake's reach.

Crack!

As you jumped, your camera strikes hard against the rocks. The lens is cracked.

You fling your legs up to safety where the snake can't reach you. The huge reptile slinks back into the marsh, and you breathe a sigh of relief.

Pythons kill their prey by wrapping their bodies around the animal and squeezing it to death.

Turn the page.

You remain on the rocks until you hear the soft hum of an airboat approaching. "Over here!" you shout, standing and waving both arms as Jim rounds a group of gnarled trees and comes into view.

"How'd it go?" he asks as you climb aboard the airboat.

"I found some handprints," you reply, showing him the photos.

"Sounds like a success," Jim says.

It's not the proof you'd hoped to find, but the photos will excite the members of BFSD. The images will increase their interest in studying the Skunk Ape.

THE END

To read another adventure, turn to page 11.
To learn more about Bigfoot, turn to page 103.

The snake is closing in on you. It's slow, though. You think you'll be able to defend yourself. You pick up a nearby rock and hold it in one hand. Then, like a major-league pitcher, you throw the rock at the reptile.

THWACK! It strikes the side of the python.

Good, you think. *That'll scare it off!*

But the rock has little effect. The snake speeds up and quickly wraps around your left ankle.

"Oh no!"

You try desperately to yank it free. But the snake is strong and won't let go. You fall over as the snake winds itself around your body. It's squeezing you tight. Unfortunately for you, there is no escape.

THE END

To read another adventure, turn to page 11.
To learn more about Bigfoot, turn to page 103.

"Will you stay here with me?" you ask. "I know you've got a business to run, but I'd love the help."

Jim nods. "Sure thing. Patty can run things while I'm out."

Jim stays and you remain on the airboat together. You hope the sound of the propeller won't scare off any Skunk Apes.

You stay near the marshland for a while, but then Jim makes a suggestion. "If we move to the right over there, we can get a better angle on the area."

"Sounds good."

The airboat stirs, then begins to slowly glide over the water and muck. Jim manoeuvres it between pockets of trees and down narrow paths in the swampland.

As you come out on the far side of the marsh, you gasp.

"Something is out there!" you whisper. A large humanlike shape has appeared behind some trees.

"Well, I'll be. . ." Jim says. "I think that's the same thing I saw before!"

You unbuckle your seat belt and lean out over the airboat's edge to take some photos. But they don't come out clearly.

"We need to get closer," you say.

Jim spurs the airboat forwards. But the shift in momentum throws you off-balance. You nearly lose your camera in the marsh. And in the effort to save it, you've lost sight of the shadowy figure.

Ahead, the marshy path splits in half. A disgusting stench fills the air. Could it be the Skunk Ape? Which way should you go?

To go left into denser glades, turn to page 66.
To go to the thinner glade area, turn to page 69.

"I didn't see where it went," Jim says quietly. It's hard to hear him over the loud noise of the airboat's propeller.

"Go left," you suggest. "I think it ran into the denser trees."

Jim turns and steers the boat in that direction.

The trees are very thick, and sometimes Jim has to steer the craft through the narrowest of waterways. Several times, tree branches scrape the side of the airboat like claws reaching out to grasp you.

Still, there is no sign of the creature.

You're disappointed. This was your big chance, and you ruined it by travelling away from the creature.

But suddenly a powerful stink drifts across the Glades. You wrinkle your nose in disgust.

"Crikey, what's that smell?" you ask.

"That's gotta be the Skunk Ape," Jim says. "You can tell by its strong stench."

"Well, then, it must be close," you reply, waving your hand in front of your face. "My eyes are watering up from that foul odour."

Jim slows the airboat. If the creature is close, you don't want to scare it.

"There!" Jim's excited voice carries out over the Glades. He's pointing straight ahead. And then you see it too. Standing in the shadows is a tall, red-brown shape.

Jim kills the airboat's engine as you swiftly take photos. The creature is hidden in the shadows, so the photos come out dark and grainy.

These photos aren't great, you think. *Maybe I should take a video instead.*

Turn the page.

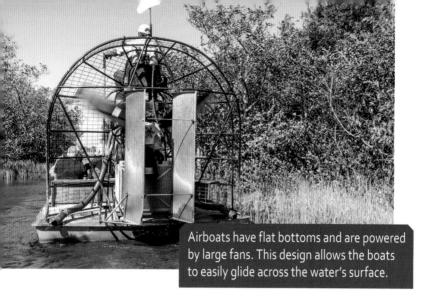

Airboats have flat bottoms and are powered by large fans. This design allows the boats to easily glide across the water's surface.

You switch the camera over to video mode and begin recording the strange creature. It's blocked by branches and is hard to see. But you whisper into the camera, "It may not be easy to see, but it's very easy to smell."

After a time, the creature drifts back into the shadows. It's gone. The video won't prove that it's a Skunk Ape. But that smell was unmistakable. You know what you've seen, even if others don't.

THE END

To read another adventure, turn to page 11.
To learn more about Bigfoot, turn to page 103.

You stand and scan the area. "Let's go to the right," you suggest. "There are fewer trees there, so it should be easier to see the creature."

Jim pilots the airboat across the more open area. But eventually, the path narrows. As Jim steers, you come across another fallen branch.

The airboat slams into the log!

Your camera flies out of your hands and lands in the marsh.

"Please don't be broken!" you hiss as you stick your hand into the muck to retrieve it.

Your wish is not granted. The mud and water have damaged your camera. Unfortunately, you will not be capturing any photo evidence of Skunk Apes on this trip.

THE END

To read another adventure, turn to page 11.
To learn more about Bigfoot, turn to page 103.

The strange tracks seen in this image taken in 1951 were thought by some to be made by a Yeti in the Himalayas.

CHAPTER 4
THE HIMALAYAN YETI

The Yeti is one of the most elusive cryptids out there. You've never travelled as far as Asia and the Himalayan Mountains before in your life.

"This opportunity is too amazing to pass up," you say. You eagerly buy your plane ticket to Nepal that night.

It's a long plane ride to Nepal. You use the time to read more information about the Yeti. The creature is also known as the Abominable Snowman. Its origins are found in the folktales of the Sherpa, some of the people native to Nepal.

Like its Bigfoot cousin, the Yeti is supposedly as tall as two metres, with brown fur. There have been many sightings and some evidence of its existence over the years.

Turn the page.

However, a lot of Yeti evidence has proved to be from other animals or, in some cases, humans.

When the plane lands, your mind is brimming with information, and you're ready to begin your search. You look out and see the beautiful mountain landscape, including Mount Everest. It takes your breath away.

You rent a rickety old car and are soon driving along winding paths. After a while you see a campsite with a small cabin and a number of tents.

A woman emerges from the cabin as you park. She's in her fifties, with deep brown skin and a plait of black hair.

"I'm Binsa Joshi," she says as you exit the car. "You must be the man searching for the Yeti."

"I am. Are you the person who reported the sighting?"

She nods. "Yes. I was guiding some hikers in the lowlands when I saw a creature of some sort. It walked upright. It might have been the Himalayan brown bear. But I have never seen a bear move like that."

You can feel your excitement building. Binsa is familiar with the animals in the area. If she isn't sure of what she saw, then perhaps a Yeti is truly roaming near by.

That evening you listen as the hikers tell their stories about exploring the mountain. Later you sleep in a tent next to theirs. The wind howls at night, and the temperatures plummet. When you wake the next morning, you bundle up against the freezing air.

"I will take you to where we saw it," Binsa says as you join her outside the tent. You shrug on your backpack and get your camera ready.

Turn the page.

"Lead the way," you say excitedly.

Binsa begins to trek out onto the snowy lowlands. You follow, your boots crunching in the snow.

It is a difficult trek. After a few hours, the cloud cover is heavy. A storm is approaching. Ahead of you is a clear stretch of snow. You can move faster there. To your right is a steeper climb up to a rocky ledge. That might provide some shelter from the storm.

To remain on the clear stretch, go to page 75.
To take the steeper climb, turn to page 86.

"Be careful on this open area," Binsa warns you. "Looks can be deceiving. There are many crevasses under the snow and ice."

You nod, wrapping your scarf tighter and continuing forwards.

The snow isn't deep, though there are many patches of ice. Your boots have good traction, and you're able to cross the thick ice easily. But then –

Crack!

You stop and look down. Beneath your feet, the ice is crisscrossed with spiderweb-like cracks.

"Don't move," Binsa says. "Who knows how deep the crevasse below us could be."

She's right. One wrong move, and you could fall through the ice!

To step off the ice, turn to page 76.
To continue forwards, turn to page 83.

The cracks under your boot widen. You can't just stay on the ice like this. You need to move. Binsa appears to be safe, so you decide that moving back to her spot is the right course of action.

You shift your weight and begin to step back toward Binsa.

"Watch out!" Binsa cries out.

CRAACK!

The ice beneath you gives way!

"Aaahhh!" you cry out. Binsa reaches for you as you pinwheel your arms. You twist your body back towards her as you start to fall.

"Grab my hand!" she shouts, thrusting an arm forwards. You try to grasp it, but you slip just out of her grasp.

You plunge down into the icy crevasse!

"Aaaahhhh!"

You fall fast, grasping at the crevasse's icy walls – at anything – to stop your fall.

"Oof!"

You slam down hard as your fall ends abruptly. Dazed, you take a moment to gather yourself and check your surroundings. You've landed on a small ledge of ice jutting out the side of the crevasse. The light above you is more than six metres away.

"Are you okay?" Binsa calls down to you.

You sit up slowly, making sure the ledge is safe. It seems to be holding you.

But how will you get out?

"I'm okay for now!" you shout back. "I don't know how long this ledge will hold me though."

"Give me a minute!" Binsa says. "I'll throw you a line."

Turn the page.

And then there is silence. You begin to shake and shudder. You're not sure if it's from the cold or from fear. It's probably both.

You wrap your arms round yourself for warmth.

"Here it comes!" From above, a thick rope begins to drop down into the crevasse. It moves slow and steady. At the end is a heavy metal carabiner, like the kind rock climbers use.

The rope sways back and forth.

You hear the icy ledge cracking beneath you. If you don't grab the rope fast, you'll plummet even further!

To reach for the rope, go to page 79.
To let the rope come to you, turn to page 80.

There's no time to lose!

You carefully slide to your knees and slowly try to stand. If you do, the rope will be within your reach.

"Lower!" you shout. "And hurry!"

"I'm doing the best I can!" Binsa replies.

It's not enough. The ice beneath you cracks. If you don't get the rope now, you never will. You quickly stand and reach up for the carabiner.

CRACK!

The icy ledge crumbles, breaking off just as your fingers graze the carabiner.

"Nooooooo!" you shout as you plummet down into the darkness.

THE END

To read another adventure, turn to page 11.
To learn more about Bigfoot, turn to page 103.

The icy shelf beneath you crackles and crumbles. You consider standing and reaching for the rope. But then you remember what happened the last time you tried to move on unstable ice. So you wait.

"Come on," you whisper. "Just a bit closer."

The rope slides further down the crevasse. You slowly reach one arm up towards it . . . so close. A chunk of the icy ledge breaks off, falling deep into the darkness below you.

"Can you reach it?" Binsa calls down to you.

You stretch your arm out, and your fingers grasp the carabiner.

"Yes!" you call back

You snatch the carabiner and hook it to your belt. And not a moment too soon! The icy ledge is crumbling all around you.

"Brace yourself!" you cry out.

Deep, dangerous crevasses in glaciers can often be hidden by thin layers of ice and snow.

The ledge breaks and falls away. The rope grows tight, leaving you dangling in mid-air. Quickly, you search for hand- and foot-holds to help hold your weight as Binsa pulls you up.

The going is slow, but eventually the top of the crevasse is in sight. You reach over the top and grab hold of solid ground. Binsa gives one last pull, and you are finally safe.

Turn the page.

"Thank you," you say, completely out of breath.

"We will have to find a better way across," Binsa says, coiling the rope and stuffing it into her backpack. She doesn't seem fazed at all that she just saved you from a terrible end.

"Just let me . . . catch my breath," you say.

Binsa glances up at the dark clouds. "If you would like to find the Yeti before that storm hits, we must move."

"Good point."

You stand and secure your pack. You gesture to Binsa. "How about you lead the way this time," you say with a slight smile.

It takes extra time, but you find a safe way across the crevasse and continue your search.

Turn to page 84.

You don't know how long the ice at your feet will hold or how deep the crevasse is under you. You can't stay where you are. It's too dangerous.

Keep moving forwards, you tell yourself.

You slowly shift your weight off your left foot, with the spiderweb cracks beneath it.

"Careful," Binsa says at your back.

The ice crackles. If you're going to move, now is the time.

You step quickly with your right foot and glide your left across the ice. Then you run as fast as you can. The ice cracks, crumbles and falls away as you run. At the last second, you leap forwards and land on the other side of the crevasse.

You're safe!

"I'll find another way across," Binsa says. You wait until she safely rejoins you.

Turn the page.

"That was more than I bargained for on this trip," you say as you and Binsa resume your hike across the lowlands.

"Mountain climbing can be dangerous," Binsa says. "I am glad you're safe."

"Thanks. Me too!"

After a while you see small pockets of trees and shrubs that dot the landscape. Snow begins to drift from the sky. As you walk past a small group of trees, you spy something near a snowy bluff in the distance. At first you think it's just an oddly-shaped rock. But then it moves!

"Look!" you whisper, bringing your camera to your eye.

"I see it," Binsa says. "We must be certain it is not a Himalayan brown bear."

"It definitely doesn't move like one," you say.

Your heartbeat quickens. The snow is growing heavier and begins to obscure the images. The creature moves across the bluff and out of sight.

You're almost certain that you've captured images of a Yeti. You turn to Binsa and suggest that you follow it.

She shakes her head and points to the clouds. "The storm is already upon us," she says. "We must return to base camp."

She's right. One life-threatening adventure is enough for today. Although the images you've taken are grainy, you can't wait to share them with the Bigfoot Field Search & Discovery people.

This has been a dangerous but successful trip!

THE END

To read another adventure, turn to page 11.
To learn more about Bigfoot, turn to page 103.

"Let's take the steeper climb," you say, pointing to the rocky bluff to your right. "There may be caves or rock ridges the creature can use to hide."

"I will lead the way," Binsa says. "But we must be careful."

Slowly, you make your way across the mountain lowlands until you reach the rocky area. Suddenly, you notice movement from the corner of your eye.

"Wait." You stop and turn. Binsa does as well. Something is moving in the nearest stand of trees.

"Over there in the trees," you whisper.

"It's a Himalayan brown bear," Binsa hisses.

And it's coming your way!

To run away, go to page 87.
To play dead, turn to page 88.

The bear lopes across the snow in your direction. Your heartbeat races.

"Whatever you do," Binsa warns you, "do not –"

"Run!" you shout. You spin around and begin to race back in the direction you came. You take a quick glance back. You see Binsa laying in the snow, curled into a ball. The bear runs past her – and heads straight for you!

"Aaagghh!" You step on an icy rock shelf and slip. Pain shoots up your leg – you've twisted your ankle. You stumble and fall.

The bear is on you in seconds. It pounces, jaws wide and teeth gleaming. This trip to the Himalayas will be your last expedition ever.

THE END

To read another adventure, turn to page 11.
To learn more about Bigfoot, turn to page 103.

"Oh no," you whisper. Your heart crashes against your ribs. Your feet feel like cement. You've never seen a bear this close.

"Whatever you do," Binsa whispers, "do not run."

"Then what do we do?" you ask.

"Lie down and pretend to be dead."

She falls to the snow and curls up in a ball. She covers her neck with her hands. You quickly do the same.

The bear still lopes towards you. You squeeze your eyes shut and hold your breath. You can hear the bear puffing and snorting as it reaches you. It bends down and presses its snout against you. You can smell its foul breath as it sniffs you. One enormous paw bats at you, striking you in the ribs. You fight the urge to yell in pain.

One wrong move, and you'll end up becoming the bear's dinner.

After what feels like forever, the bear steps over you and continues on its way. You peel open your eyes. Binsa is sitting up, a smile on her face. "Well done," she says. "That was quite an experience."

"That's an understatement," you say, trying hard to stop shaking.

Binsa leads the way again, heading through the rocky lowlands. Snow begins to fall. Soon it will be a steady storm, but there's still time to try to capture some images. Ahead, the path splits in two. To the left are a series of caves. To the right, the rocks turn into a cliff. Which direction will you tell Binsa to go?

To go left towards the caves, turn to page 90.
To go right towards the cliff, turn to page 100.

The cliffs are closer, but the caves are more appealing. "If a Yeti is hiding out in the lowlands," you say, "that's where it'd be."

Binsa leads you in the direction of the caves. It's slow going. The snow is deeper here. At times, the drifts come up to your knees.

Ahead, there are several caves in the side of the mountain. They're surrounded by a thick stand of trees. The spindly pines twist up into the sky like guards watching over the caves. Or more accurately, guarding anything that lives in the caves.

As you get nearer, a shape appears in the trees.

"There!" you whisper, pointing.

This is no brown bear. Whatever you're seeing in the trees is tall, with red-brown fur. It's hard to be sure from this distance, but you're nearly certain it's a Yeti.

You snap photos of the creature as it moves through the trees towards the nearest cave. Fat flakes of snow drift from the sky.

"A storm is coming," Binsa warns you. "We must go back soon."

You check your camera's view screen. The photos of the creature are foggy and unclear thanks to the snow. You look up in time to see the shape disappear into the cave.

"We can't go back until I get a clear shot," you explain.

Binsa shakes her head. "It's too dangerous."

You understand what Binsa is saying. But if you follow the creature to the caves, you'd have shelter and get better images.

To follow the shape into the caves, turn to page 92.
To head back towards camp, turn to page 94.

You look up at the sky, watching the snow fall.

"I don't have a good enough photo yet," you say. "I'm heading into the cave."

"Then we must make it quick," Binsa says.

"Okay."

When you reach the cave entrance, you look in the snow for any good prints. But the area is packed down. There are no clear Yeti prints.

Cautiously, you enter the cave.

Entering a dark, icy mountain cave can be dangerous. A person may be buried in snow or ice or attacked by a wild animal.

It's dark in the cave. It stinks like the remains of dead animals. You feel like this was a mistake. You turn to flee when you hear a sound in front of you.

A shadow descends on you, followed by a low, guttural growl.

You take a photo, and your flash blazes brightly in the darkness. In front of you, seen briefly in the glare, is a beast unlike anything you've seen before.

The creature swats at you, knocking the camera from your hands. It shatters against the cave wall.

"Run, Binsa!" you shout, turning for the cave entrance.

The beast grabs your thick coat with its powerful claw-like hand.

There's no escape.

THE END

To read another adventure, turn to page 11.
To learn more about Bigfoot, turn to page 103.

You flip through your images. They don't show much, but they may be the only ones you'll get. The snow is falling in thick flakes. If Binsa says it's going to be a full-on storm, you trust her.

But still, you feel this is your best chance to get evidence of the Yeti.

You shake your head. "You're right," you say. "We should head back to camp. But can we give it five more minutes? Maybe it'll come out of the cave."

Binsa nods. "Five minutes, no more."

You train your camera at the cave and wait.

No luck.

Binsa shakes your shoulder. "We must go now if we wish to return safely to base camp."

You reluctantly agree.

Whatever is in that cave will have to remain a mystery.

You begin your trek back to base camp. But the snow has picked up and makes the trip back difficult. Snowflakes cling to your woolly hat, your coat and your face.

"We're . . . not going to make it back," Binsa says. She points ahead, and all you see is snow. "The conditions are a near whiteout. We could find ourselves heading in the wrong direction."

"Then what should we do?" you ask.

"We either press on," she says, "or we build a shelter and wait out the storm. What would you like to do?"

Both ideas sound dangerous. But Binsa is waiting for your reply.

To press on towards camp, turn to page 96.
To build a shelter, turn to page 98.

You squint into the distance. It's snowing hard. But camp can't be that far away, can it?

"I think we should continue on," you say. "It's better to go back to camp than to be in this storm all night. We've still got plenty of daylight."

Binsa tightens her scarf. "Okay," she says. "We'll continue forwards."

She takes out a compass and studies it. Then she points to the left.

Weather can be unpredictable in the mountains. Sudden winter storms may strike without warning, causing hikers or climbers to become lost.

"Camp should be that way," she says, trudging forwards through the snow drifts.

After a while daylight fades into darkness. You feel the deep chill of night creeping into your hands and feet. There is no base camp in sight.

Binsa staggers and stops. She shakes her head. "I don't . . . get it," she says, huffing. "We should . . . be at camp . . . by now."

Binsa checks her compass again and changes your direction. You continue to hike through the night. By the time you decide to build a shelter, it's too late. Your camera is frozen, and so are you. When you finally reach camp the following morning, you are suffering from severe frostbite. You've survived, but at a price. And you have no evidence of the Yeti.

THE END

To read another adventure, turn to page 11.
To learn more about Bigfoot, turn to page 103.

You glance to the sky, watching as the thick flakes wind down from the clouds. Ahead, you can barely see where you're going. It's getting dangerous to continue forward.

"You think building a shelter is the best course of action?" you ask Binsa.

She nods.

"Then let's do it."

Together, you fall to your knees and begin to scoop snow out of the nearest drift. Heavy clumps fall away, and before long you've carved an igloo-like shape in the drift. It's just large enough to fit both of you as you climb in together and huddle close.

You stay that way for the night. It's cold and you get little rest but being huddled together for warmth has probably saved your lives.

When morning arrives the sun cuts across the snowy landscape. You push your way out of the shelter. You're stiff and sore, but you've survived the night.

In the gleaming, brilliant morning light, Binsa is able to safely guide you back to the base camp.

"We made it!" you say, hugging her when you see the tents and cabin in the distance.

You hope the weather has not affected your camera too badly. The images, while blurry and foggy, may be just enough to prove the Yeti's existence. It's up to others to study and judge your photos. And you're content with that.

THE END

To read another adventure, turn to page 11.
To learn more about Bigfoot, turn to page 103.

The caves are appealing, but the cliff is closer. And you have a good feeling about it.

"Let's head that way," you suggest, pointing at the cliffs.

"We must be careful," Binsa says.

You make your way towards the cliffs. Several times, you find yourself slipping on the rocks.

Maybe coming this way wasn't such a good idea, you think. But still, you trudge on.

As you near the cliffs, you spy something on the ground. It is the remains of a small animal. Chunks of meat still cling to the bones. The kill is fresh.

"Something is close," you say, glancing round.

You don't see anything moving, but you do see something on a nearby jagged rock.

"Look!" You dash to the rock but pull up short. There in the snow at your feet is a large footprint!

"This is amazing!" you say, taking a series of photos.

You turn your attention to the rock, carefully moving around the footprint. A clump of red-brown fur clings to the jagged stone. It looks like it got caught on the rock and was pulled off whatever creature it belonged to.

"This could be Yeti fur!" you tell Binsa, taking more photos and a video of the area.

"Come on!" Binsa waves to you. "You have your proof. Let us return to camp before we get caught out in the storm!"

You follow her, happy with your trip's find. You can't wait to share your evidence of the Yeti with BFSD.

THE END

To read another adventure, turn to page 11.
To learn more about Bigfoot, turn to page 103.

Explorer C. Thomas Biscardi took this photo of a supposed Bigfoot in northern California in 1981.

CHAPTER 5

BIGFOOT: REAL OR HOAX?

The legend of Bigfoot has been around for many years. In North American folklore, Bigfoot (or Sasquatch) creatures are often portrayed as the missing link between humans and other great apes. They're said to be hairy, ape-like creatures that walk upright and live in the wilderness.

But do they truly exist?

Fossil evidence shows that a similar creature did exist about one to nine million years ago. It was called *Gigantopithecus*. Not much is known about the creature. But it was larger than a gorilla and had teeth similar to a human's. The *Gigantopithecus's* closest living relative is the orangutan. These great apes share many of the same features that witnesses have described about Bigfoot.

There have been many notable sightings of Bigfoot over the years. One of the most important occurred in 1955, when William Roe claimed to have seen the creature. Roe said he was hiking when he came across the animal. He hid in the bushes to watch it. He described it as being an ape-like creature. Roe's encounter became one of the first tales of the modern Bigfoot.

The most famous image of Bigfoot comes from the 1967 film made by Roger Patterson and Bob Gimlin. In the film, an unknown creature strides across a gravel sand bar and passes behind some logs. The creature seems to look directly back at the camera as it disappears into the woods.

Nobody knows if the Patterson–Gimlin film is real. There have been many hoaxes over the years. For sceptics, most film and video evidence of Bigfoot is obviously just a person in a gorilla suit.

Of the many Bigfoot hoaxes, the most common are reported discoveries of Bigfoot's "footprints". The supposed footprint evidence goes as far back as 1958. A journalist claimed to find puzzling giant footprints and made plaster casts of them.

Since then, hundreds of Bigfoot's prints have been reported by searchers. They've also claimed to have found samples of Bigfoot hair and scat (poo). But DNA tests have always shown that the samples come from various wild animals.

Many sceptics think Bigfoot's existence won't be proved until one is either captured or killed. Does Bigfoot truly exist? We may never know!

Bigfoot around the world

Native people of North America have told tales of Sasquatch creatures for hundreds of years. But tales of Bigfoot, Yeti and similar creatures are found all over the world. Are the creatures real? Nobody knows for sure. Only one thing is certain: people are seeing something that they can't explain.

Bigfoot (northern California):

Roger Patterson and Robert Gimlin encountered and filmed a Bigfoot in northern California in 1967. It became the most famous Bigfoot sighting ever.

Ucu (Argentina):

This Bigfoot-like creature is reported to live in the Andes Mountains. It's about the size of a large dog and its call sounds like *uhu, uhu*.

Skunk Ape (Florida Everglades):

Florida's famous Skunk Ape is said to be more than 2 metres (7 ft) tall. Witnesses say it smells like a combination of rotten eggs, mouldy cheese and dung.

Moehau (New Zealand):

Tales of this creature were first told by the Maori people. The "wild man of the woods" was described with shaggy yellow hair and large tusks.

Urayuli (Alaska):

The Yup'ik people in south-west Alaska have long told tales of the Urayuli. It's described as being 3 metres (10 ft) tall with glowing eyes and extra-long arms.

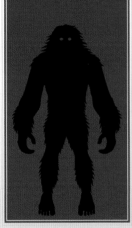

Big Greyman (Scotland):

This extremely tall creature reportedly lives among the tallest mountains of Scotland. Tales of these creatures go as far back as the 1200s.

Yeti (Nepal/Tibet):

Also known as the Abominable Snowman, the Yeti is said to live in the Himalayan Mountains. Native people of Nepal and Tibet have told tales of the Yeti for hundreds of years.

Yowie (Australia):

The Yowie is said to roam in the wilderness of Australia. It is similar to both Bigfoot in North America and the Yeti in the Himalayas.

Orang Pendak (Indonesia):

This animal has been reported in Indonesia for more than 100 years. It stands from 80 to 150 centimetres (31 to 59 in) tall. Some people believe it may be an ape similar to an orangutan.

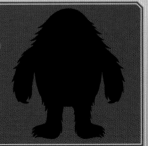

Glossary

airboat small, shallow boat driven by a large, caged propeller at the rear that pushes the boat through swamps and marshes

carabiner oval-shaped metal clip; climbers use carabiners to secure rope to ice anchors.

compass instrument used for finding directions while travelling

crevasse deep, wide crack in a glacier or ice sheet

cryptid animal or creature that people have claimed to see but there is no proof it exists

cryptozoology study of evidence for unproven creatures such as Bigfoot or the Loch Ness monster

elusive clever at hiding

evidence information, items and facts that help prove something to be true or false

evolution gradual change of living things over long periods of time

folktale tale or story passed down from previous generations that is often based on superstitions

gene part of every cell that determines characteristics passed from parents to their offspring

hoax trick to make people believe something that is not true

lope move or run with a long, easy stride

marsh area of wet, low land usually covered in grasses and low plants

plaster cast mould of an object made out of a hard substance that contains lime, sand and water

primate any member of the group of mammals that includes humans, apes and monkeys

putrid having the odour of decaying flesh

scat animal droppings

sceptic person who questions things that other people believe in

Other paths to explore

>>> While searching for Bigfoot, you often encounter dangerous animals in the wilderness. What can you do to prepare for these encounters? What kit can you take to stay safe? What actions can you take to either avoid a wild animal or defend yourself if one attacks?

>>> You've gone on the hunt for three well-known Bigfoot creatures. But there are reports of several similar creatures around the world. Look at the descriptions on pages 106–107. Which mysterious creature would you like to search for next? Think about what part of the world you would be travelling to. What preparations would you need to make to help your search be successful?

>>> Evidence of Bigfoot is mostly limited to some blurry photos and videos, footprint moulds and some hair samples. But none of these are enough to prove that Bigfoot is real. If you went on a hunt for Bigfoot, what other evidence would you look for to prove whether or not the creature exists?

Find out more

Bigfoot (Monster Histories), Bradley Cole (Raintree, 2020)

Cryptids (Guidebooks to the Unexplained), Kenny Abdo (Calico Kid, 2020)

kids.kiddle.co/Bigfoot
Visit this website for some Bigfoot facts.

www.bbc.co.uk/newsround/26050829
Find out more about Bigfoot, the Loch Ness Monster and other mysterious cryptids with Newsround.

Brandon Terrell (1978–2021)
Brandon was a passionate reader and Star Wars fan, amazing father, son, uncle, friend and devoted husband. Brandon received his undergraduate degree from the Minneapolis College of Art and Design and his Master of Fine Arts in Writing for Children and Young Adults from Hamline University in St. Paul, Minnesota, USA. Brandon was a talented storyteller, writing more than 100 books for children in his career. This book is dedicated to his memory. Happy reading!

Index